Islamic Studies

Grade 3

Given the dire need of Islamic studies material in schools incorporating the subject in English, Darussalam has endeavoured to publish an Islamic Studies series covering all the grades, from grade one through grade twelve.

© **Maktaba Dar-us-Salam, 2009**
King Fahd National library Cataloging-in-Publication Data
Abdul aziz, Moulavi

Islamic Studies - grade 3	Moulavi Abdul aziz - Riyadh 2009
114p : 29cm	**ISBN : 978-9960-500-16-4**
1-Islam 2-Islam - General principles	1-Title
210 dc	1430/3519
L.D. No. 1430/3519	**ISBN : 978-9960-500-16-4**

Supervised by:

Abdul Malik Mujahid

HEAD OFFICE

P.O. Box: 22743, Riyadh 11416 K.S.A.Tel: 0096 -1-4033962/4043432 Fax: 4021659
E-mail: darussalam@awalnet.net.sa, riyadh@dar-us-salam.com Website: www.dar-us-salam.com

K.S.A. Darussalam Showrooms:
Riyadh
Olaya branch: Tel 00966-1-4614483 Fax: 4644945
Malaz branch: Tel 00966-1-4735220 Fax: 4735221
Suwailam branch: Tel & Fax-1-2860422

- **Jeddah**
  Tel: 00966-2-6879254 Fax: 6336270
- **Madinah**
  Tel: 00966-503417155 Fax: 04-8151121
- **Al-Khobar**
  Tel: 00966-3-8692900 Fax: 8691551
- **Khamis Mushayt**
  Tel & Fax: 00966-072207055
- **Yanbu Al-Bahr** Tel: 0500887341 Fax: 04-3908027
- **Al-Buraida** Tel: 0503417156 Fax: 063696124

U.A.E
- **Darussalam, Sharjah U.A.E**
  Tel: 00971-6-5632623 Fax: 5632624
  Sharjah@dar-us-salam.com.

PAKISTAN
- **Darussalam, 36 B Lower Mall, Lahore**
  Tel: 0092-42-724 0024 Fax: 7354072
- **Rahman Market, Ghazni Street,**Urdu Bazar Lahore
  Tel: 0092-42-7120054 Fax: 7320703
- **Karachi,** Tel: 0092-21-4393936 Fax: 4393937
- **Islamabad,** Tel: 0092-51-2500237 Fax: 512281513

U.S.A
- **Darussalam, Houston**
  P.O Box: 79194 Tx 77279
  Tel: 001-713-722 0419 Fax: 001-713-722 0431
  E-mail: houston @dar-us-salam.com
- **Darussalam, New York** 486 Atlantic Ave, Brooklyn
  New York-11217, Tel: 001-718-625 5925
  Fax: 718-625 1511
  E-mail: darussalamny@hotmail.com

U.K
- **Darussalam International Publications Ltd.**
  Leyton Business Centre
  Unit-17, Etloe Road, Leyton, London, E10 7BT
  Tel: 0044 20 8539 4885 Fax:0044 20 8539 4889
  Website: www.darussalam.com
  Email: info@darussalam.com
- **Darussalam International Publications Limited**
  Regents Park Mosque, 146 Park Road
  London NW8 7RG Tel: 0044- 207 725 2246
  Fax: 0044 20 8539 4889

AUSTRALIA
- **Darussalam**: 153, Haldon St, Lakemba (Sydney)
  NSW 2195, Australia
  Tel: 0061-2-97407188 Fax: 0061-2-97407199
  Mobile: 0061-414580813 Res: 0061-2-97580190
  Email: abumuaaz@hotamail.com

CANADA
- **Islmic Books Service**
  2200 South Sheridan way Mississauga,
  Ontario Canada L5K 2C8
  Tel:001-905-403-8406 Ext. 218 Fax: 905-8409

HONG KONG
- **Peacetech**
  A2, 4/F Tsim Sha Mansion
  83-87 Nathan Road Tsimbatsui
  Kowloon, Hong Kong
  Tel: 00852 2369 2722 Fax: 00852-23692944
  Mobile: 00852 97123624

MALAYSIA
- **Darussalam International Publication Ltd.**
  No.109A, Jalan SS 21/1A, Damansara Utama,
  47400, Petaling Jaya, Selangor, Darul Ehsan, Malaysia
  Tel: 00603 7710 9750 Fax: 7710 0749
  E-mail: darussalm@streamyx.com

FRANCE
- **Editions & Librairie Essalam**
  135, Bd de Ménilmontant- 75011 Paris
  Tél: 0033-01- 43 38 19 56/ 44 83
  Fax: 0033-01-43 57 44 31
  E-mail: essalam@essalam com·

SINGAPORE
- Muslim Converts Association of Singapore
  32 Onan Road The Galaxy
  Singapore- 424484
  Tel: 0065-440 6924, 348 8344 Fax: 440 6724

SRI LANKA
- Darul Kitab 6, Nimal Road, Colombo-4
  Tel: 0094 115 358712 Fax: 115-358713

INDIA
- Islamic Books International
  54, Tandel Street (North)
  Dongri, Mumbai 4000 09,
  Tel: 0091-22-2373 4180, Fax: 0091-22-2373 0689
  E-mail: sales@irf.net

SOUTH AFRICA
- Islamic Da`wah Movement (IDM)
  48009 Qualbert 4078 Durban,South Africa
  Tel: 0027-31-304-6883 Fax: 0027-31-305-1292
  E-mail: idm@ion.co.za

All praise belongs to Allah; we praise Him and seek His help and forgiveness. We seek refuge in Allah from the evil of our own selves and from our sinful deeds. Whomever Allah guides, there is none to misguide him; and whomever He leads astray, none can guide him. We bear witness that there is no god worthy of worship except Allah, alone, and we bear witness that Muhammad is His servant and Messenger. We pray to Allah the Almighty to bestow His peace and blessings upon Prophet Muhammad, upon his good and pure family, as well as upon all the noble companions and those who follow them in righteousness until the Day of Judgement.

Given the dire need for Islamic studies material in schools incorporating the subject in English, Darussalam has endeavoured to publish an Islamic Studies series covering all the grades, from grade one through grade twelve.

The present series covers all areas of Islamic studies: *tafseer, hadeeth, tawheed, fiqh, seerah,* and general etiquette relating to different areas and situations. Given the importance of authentic Islamic knowledge, every effort has been made to ensure that the material presented in the series is authentic. Also, given the importance of Arabic Islamic terms, most of the terms are presented in their original Arabic script, along with the transliteration and the translation of their meanings. This also applies to supplications which have to be memorised in their Arabic version. The aim here is to help the reader read the original text and understand its meaning. Each lesson is followed by exercises covering questions about the lesson.

One striking feature in the series is the colourful artwork used in it that certainly appeals to children. This is certainly bound to attract the young readers' attention, stimulate them, amuse them as well as educate them.

The series aims to acquaint the student with the teachings of Islam in every aspect: beliefs, practices and moral conduct. The series, with its unique features, certainly fills a gap in this area which has long been partially neglected.

The present breathtaking work was initiated by an expert in the field of education, Maulvi Abdul Aziz, MA. English literature, who held different posts in the field including that of Senior Administrative Officer in the Department of Private Education, Ministry of Education, Dubai, UAE, from 1982 to 2002.

The current project also owes its existence in its present form to a number of people who made informative suggestions, particularly Al-Arabee Ben Razzouq, College of Languages and Translation, Imam Muhammad ibn Saud University, Riyadh, who undertook the painstaking task of checking the authenticity of the material presented in the series, proofreading the text as well as adding references to certain quotations from the Qur'an and the *hadeeth*. Special thanks also go to Sheikh Abdul-Qawiy Luqman, Al-Madeenah University graduate, for his interesting suggestions and to Mr. Zulfiqar Mahmood who conscientiously applied his expertise in the field of graphic design to produce the series in a superb shape.

We pray to Almighty Allah to reward our endeavours and to make the present series abundantly beneficial to students in all stages of education as well as to any one who reads them.

Abdul Malik Mujahid
Jumaada al-Ukhra, 1430 AH.
June 2009.

CONTENTS

1

Chapter

The Mu'adh-dhin calls out the adhan five times a day at the mosque. The mu'adh-dhin is the person who calls the adhan - the call to prayer. If you climb a city rooftop at the time of any of the five daily prayers, you can hear several calls, with long sweeping voices coming in from different directions. The call to prayer is one of the most beautiful sounds. It is delightful to wake to the sound of the dawn adhan, or hear the Isha adhan when the evening is cool and gentle.

The call to prayer punctuates daily life five times. It draws Muslims out of their everyday activities to matters of great importance - salah.

The wording of the adhan is:

اَللهُ أَكْبَر   اَللهُ أَكْبَر

Allaahu Akbar, Allaahu Akbar
Allah is Most Great, Allah is Most Great

اَللهُ أَكْبَر   اَللهُ أَكْبَر

Allaahu Akbar, Allaahu Akbar
Allah is Most Great, Allah is Most Great

أَشْهَدُ أَنْ لَا إِلَهَ إِلاَّ الله

ash-hadu an laa-ilaaha illallaah
I testify that there is no god but Allah

أَشْهَدُ أَنْ لَا إِلَهَ إِلاَّ الله

ash-hadu an laa-ilaaha illallaah
I testify that there is no god but Allah

أَشْهَدُ أَنَّ مُحَمَّدًا رَسُولُ الله

ash-hadu anna muhammadar-rasoolullaah
I testify that Muhammad is the Messenger of Allah

أَشْهَدُ أَنَّ مُحَمَّدًا رَسُولُ الله

ash-hadu anna muhammadar-rasoolullaah
I testify that Muhammad is the Messenger of Allah

حَيَّ عَلىالصَّلَاة   حَيَّ عَلىالصَّلَاة

hayya alassalaah, hayya alassalaah
Hasten to the prayer, hasten to the prayer

حَيَّ عَلىالْفَلَاح   حَيَّ عَلىالْفَلَاح

hayya alal falaah, hayya alal falaah
Hasten to success, hasten to success

اَللهُ أَكْبَر   اَللهُ أَكْبَر

Allaahu Akbar, Allaahu Akbar
Allah is Most Great, Allah is Most Great

لَا إِلَهَ إِلاَّ الله

Laa-ilaaha illallaah
There is no god but Allah

After saying

حَيَّ عَلَى الصَّلَاة   حَيَّ عَلَى الصَّلَاة

hayya alassalaah, hayya alassalaah
Hasten to the prayer, hasten to the prayer

حَيَّ عَلَى الْفَلَاح   حَيَّ عَلَى الْفَلَاح

hayya alal falaah, hayya alal falaah
Hasten to success, hasten to success

the mu'adh-dhin adds the following statement twice in the dawn prayer:

اَلصَّلَاةُ خَيْرٌ مِنَ النَّوْم

Assalaatu khayrum-minan nawm
The prayer is better than sleep

As the mu'adh-dhin calls the adhan, a Muslim should repeat after him whatever he says, except for these two statements:

حَيَّ عَلَى الصَّلَاة   حَيَّ عَلَى الصَّلَاة

hayya alassalaah, hayya alassalaah
Hasten to the prayer, hasten to the prayer

حَيَّ عَلَى الْفَلَاح   حَيَّ عَلَى الْفَلَاح

hayya alal falaah, hayya alal falaah
Hasten to success, hasten to success

Instead, one should say after each one of these statements,

لَاحَوْلَ وَلَاقُوَّةَ إِلَّا بِالله

Laa hawla wa laa quwwata illaa billaah.
There is no power and no might except with Allah

Allah's Messenger (ﷺ) said, "When you hear the adhan, repeat what the mu'adh-dhin says".(Al-Bukhaaree and Muslim)

Exercises

Exercise 1

Fill in the blanks.

1. The mu'adh-dhin calls out the _____ five times a day. Muslims then get ready to offer _____.

2. When you hear the adhan you should prepare yourself for
    _____.

Exercise 2

Learn the wording of the adhan by heart.

Chapter 2

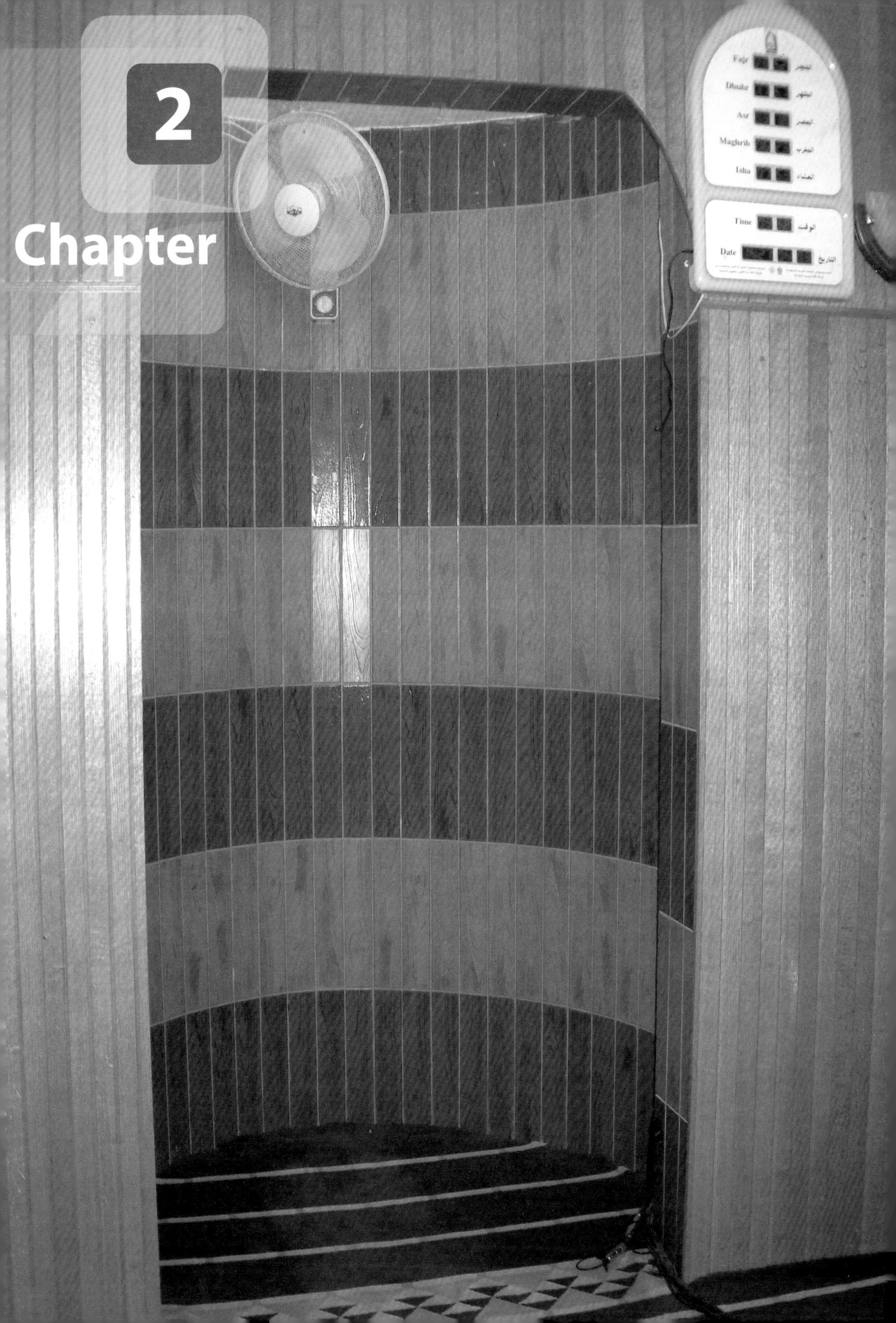
Fajr الفجر
Dhuhr الظهر
Asr العصر
Maghrib المغرب
Isha العشاء
Time الوقت
Date التاريخ

Al-iqamah is the call to the start of fard salah. A person praying alone may recite it quietly to himself or herself when they stand to offer any of the five daily prayers.

Al-iqamah is the message that the prayer is starting. One should now join the jamaa'ah and stand facing the qiblah to begin the prayer.

The wording of the iqamah is as follows:

اَللّٰهُ أَكْبَرُ اَللّٰهُ أَكْبَرُ

Allaahu Akbar, Allaahu Akbar
Allah is Most Great, Allah is Most Great

أَشْهَدُ أَنْ لَا إِلٰهَ إِلاَّ اللّٰهُ

ash-hadu an laa-ilaaha illallaah
I testify that there is no god but Allah

أَشْهَدُ أَنَّ مُحَمَّدًا رَسُولُ اللّٰهِ

ash-hadu anna muhammadar-rasoolullaah
I testify that Muhammad is the Messenger of Allah

حَيَّ عَلى الْفَلَاح   حَيَّ عَلى الصَّلَاة

hayya alassalaah, hayya alal falaah

Hasten to the prayer, hasten to success

قَدْ قَامَتِ الصَّلَاة   قَدْ قَامَتِ الصَّلَاة

Qad qaamatis-salaah, Qad qaamatis-salaah

The prayer is now ready, the prayer is now ready

اَللهُ أَكْبَر اَللهُ أَكْبَر

Allaahu Akbar, Allaahu Akbar

Allah is Most Great, Allah is Most Great

لَا إِلَهَ إِلَّا الله

Laa-ilaaha illallaah

There is no god but Allah

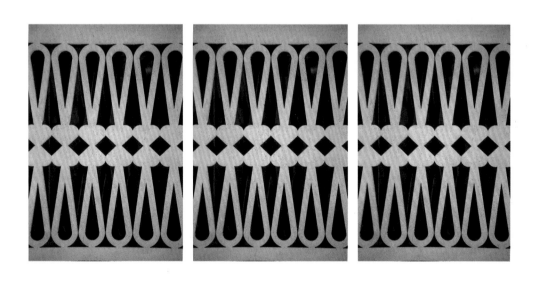

Exercises

Exercise 1

Answer the following questions

1. What is the iqamah?

   _____

   _____

2. How is it different from the adhan?

   _____

   _____

   _____

Exercise 2

Learn the iqamah with its meanings.

3
Chapter

The tongue is one of the most useful parts of the body. We use it to express our needs, wants and ideas. But if we are not careful, we can easily use it in the wrong way. The tongue is a great blessing from Allah. Even though it is small, it is too difficult to control.

A good Muslim must try hard to use his tongue only in matters that are pleasing to Allah. He must also try his best to avoid using it in such bad things as lying, gossiping and backbiting.

Gossiping and Backbiting

To gossip means to talk about other people's private lives which might be unkind or not true. This is perhaps the most difficult thing to control. It is easy to make fun of others. It is easy to nudge a friend with your elbow to get a giggle. But it is good to remember that if we do not have anything nice to say, then we should not say anything at all.

Our Prophet (ﷺ) once said, '(The true) Muslim is the one who avoids harming Muslims with his tongue and hands.' (Al-Bukharee and Muslim)

He also said, 'Do you know what backbiting is?' The Prophet's companions said, 'Allah and His Messenger know best.' Then he said, 'Backbiting is your talking about your brother in a manner that he does not like.' This means when he is not with you.

Telling Lies

For many people, lying is the quickest and safest way to get out of trouble. But in the long run lying always lands us into trouble – more trouble!

When you get caught lying, which you most likely will, you would be in much more trouble than you were when you started lying. No one likes to be lied to. Lying is lying! It does not matter if we lie about where we were, what we did, who we saw or what we saw; for we will be questioned about this on the Day of Judgement.

Lying is a very bad habit that attracts nothing but more lies. The more people ask you to talk, the more stories you make up. The more stories you make up, the deeper you land into trouble. We should, therefore, always speak the truth, and never lie.

Exercises

Exercise 1

Match the terms to their meanings and copy them in your exercise books.

1.	Lying	to talk about other people's private lives which might be unkind or not true.
2.	Gossiping	To talk about your Muslim brother or sister who is not there in a manner he or she does not like.
3.	Backbiting	To say things that are not true.

Exercises

Exercice 2

Are these statements true or false?

1.   It is OK to lie while joking. _____

2.   It is OK to lie sometimes. _____

3.   Lying is a way to get out of trouble _____

Exercise 3

Answer this question.

Who is a true Muslim?

_____

_____

_____

Salah (the prayer) is the second pillar of Islam. It is the foundation of religion and the best act of obedience. There are five prayers which Allah has prescribed for His servants.

Allah's Messenger (‎) said, 'If there is a river at the door of any one of you in which he washes himself five times a day, would any dirt remain on his body?' when his companions replied, 'None at all', the Prophet (‎) said, 'That is like the five prayers by which Allah removes sins.' (Al-Bukhaaree)

After the affirmation of Allah's Oneness, no duty that Allah has prescribed for His servants is dearer to Him than performing the obligatory prayers.

Allah's Messenger (ﷺ) said, 'The merit of the congregational prayer - jamaa'ah - surpasses that of the individual prayer by twenty-seven degrees.'

(Al-Bukhaaree and Muslim)

The Prophet (ﷺ) also said, 'To perform the late evening prayer (Isha) in congregation is equivalent to spending half the night in prayer, and to perform the dawn prayer (Fajr) in congregation is like spending the whole night in prayer.' (At-Tirmidhee)

Salah is so important in Islam that we are ordered to perform it whether we are travelling or not, and whether we are in a state of safety or danger. It is compulsory upon every sane, adult Muslim. None of the five daily prayers (salawaat – plural of salah) should be neglected. If someone is too ill to stand, then he should pray sitting. If he is too ill to sit, then he should pray lying down.

Exercises

Exercise 1

Fill in the blanks.

1. Salah is the _____ pillar of Islam.

2. A Muslim must pray _____ times a day.

3. The five prayers remove _____ just as water removes dirt.

4. The merit of the congregational prayer is _____ times more than the individual prayer.

5. Salah should not be neglected. If someone is too ill to stand, he should pray _____. If he is too ill to sit, he should pray _____.

Exercise 2

Answer the following questions.

1. What are the five prayers compared to?

    _____

    _____

2. What did the Prophet (ﷺ) say the performance of the Isha and Fajr prayers in congregation are equal to?

    _____

    _____

5

Chapter

Zakah is the third pillar of Islam. The Qur'an mentions it immediately after the prayer, saying, 'And offer prayer and give zakah.' (73:20)

Zakah is an Arabic word. It is an amount of alms which must be paid by every Muslim who possesses a certain amount of wealth. The root meaning of the Arabic term suggests that it is a means of purification and growth. Hence Zakah means purifying dues. Man loves worldly goods and wealth because these are the means by which he can enjoy the benefits of this world. Because of these worldly goods, man becomes so attached to life that he hates death.

Allah, therefore, puts Muslims to the test. He commands them to give up some of their wealth, which they love dearly.

Zakah is mentioned many times in the Qu'ran. It is compulsory for those Muslims who have wealth. It is for the benefit of those who are poor or in need. It also cleanses and purifies the giver. It makes the person who gives it aware that he should not be selfish with what Allah has given him. Zakah also benefits the whole society. It makes ties of brotherhood between the rich and the poor much stronger.

Allah's Messenger (ﷺ) said, "Whoever is given wealth by Allah and does not give the zakah due on it will find that on the Day of judgement it is made to appear to him as a hairless snake with two black specks, which chains him, and then seizes him by his jaw and says,' I'm your wealth, I'm your treasure."

(Al-Bukhaaree)

You will learn about zakah in detail later on, inshaa Allah.

Exercises

Exercise 1

Choose from the following words and fill in the blanks.

[third, Qur'an, wealth, purifies, Arabic]

1. Zakah is mentioned many times in the _____.

2. It is the _____ pillar of Islam.

3. It is compulsory for those who have _____.

4. Zakah cleanses and _____ the person who gives it.

5. It is an _____ term.

Exercise 2

Answer the following question.

Write down two benefits of giving zakah.

_____

_____

_____

6

Chapter

Sawm, or siyyaam, is an Arabic word which means fasting. Fasting is compulsory for adult Muslims throughout the month of Ramadan. Ramadan is the ninth month in the Islamic calendar. It comes after Sha'ban. Fasting in the month of Ramadan is the fourth pillar of Islam.

Fasting means abstaining from food and drink and other things that make fasting invalid from dawn to sunset. If you abstain from something, usually something you want to do or have, you do not do it even if you like to do it or have it.

Fasting also means keeping one's ears, eyes, tongue, hands and feet – and all the other parts of the body – free from sin, free from disobeying Allah and free from harming others. Backbiting or telling lies spoils the fast. Fasting is like a shield. So when a Muslim is fasting he should not use foul or foolish talk. If someone attacks him, quarrels with him or insults him, he should say, 'I'm fasting, I'm fasting.'

The fast of Ramadan begins on the day following the sighting of the new moon of the month of

Ramadan. If it is confirmed that the moon has been sighted, a Muslim should begin his fast from dawn the following day. He must make the intention of fasting (the niyyah) before dawn.

It is recommended for a Muslim to have a meal before dawn. This meal is called sahoor. It helps bear the hardships of fasting during the day. As soon as the sun has set, a Muslim should break his fast. This is called iftar – breaking the fast. He may break the fast with a few dates or other fruit or simply with water! Fasting is compulsory in the month of Ramadan for every adult Muslim who is in good health, not travelling and able to fast without hardship. An adult is a mature, well-developed person.

Exercises

Exercise 1

Circle the correct answer.

1. Sawm is an [Arabic – English] word.

2. Fasting is compulsory for [adults – children].

3. Ramadan is the [10th – 9th] month in the Islamic calendar.

4. Ramadan comes after [Shawwal – Sha'ban].

5. Ramadan is the [fifth – fourth] pillar of Islam.

Exercise 2

Write a short note on things you should keep away from while fasting.

_____

_____

_____

_____

Exercises

Exercise 3

Fill in the blanks.

1. Muslims fast from _____ until _____.

2. Breaking the fast is called _____.

3. We may break our fast with _____ or other fruit, or simply with _____.

Exercise 4

Write True or False.

1. It is recommended to eat or drink something before dawn. _____

2. Making the intention before fasting is important. _____

3. If someone insults you while you are fasting, you should insult him. _____

7
Chapter

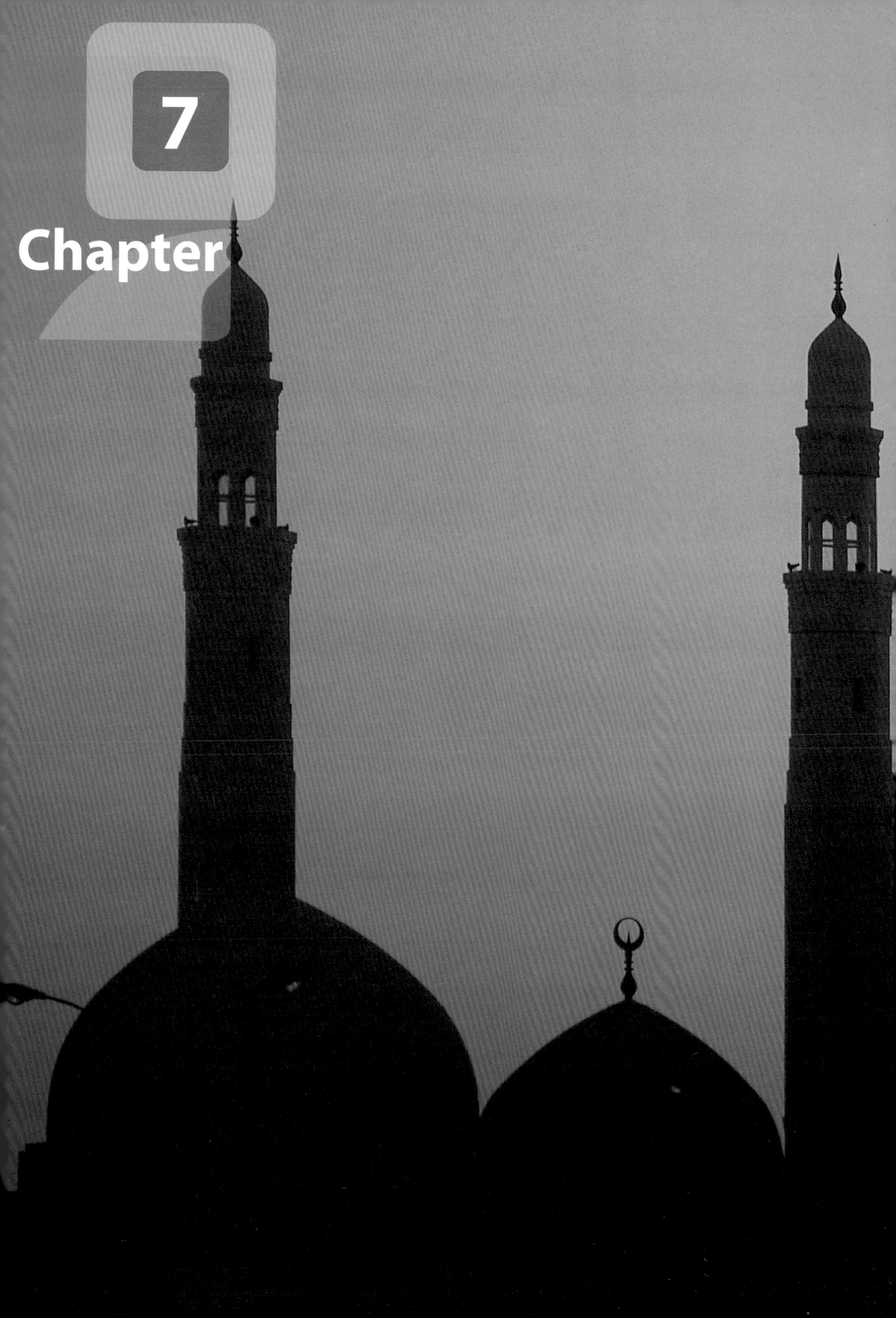

For one month every year, Muslims show their thankfulness to Allah in a special way: They fast during the month of Ramadan.

Fasting in this month is the fourth pillar of Islam. As the Islamic calendar follows the moon, the month of Ramadan falls at a different time each year.

There are several reasons for keeping this fast. The most important of them all is that it is the Command of Allah to do so. It is one of the pillars of Islam. It helps us become pious. It is the teaching of our Prophet Muhammad (ﷺ). Fasting reminds Muslims of the hardships of the poor.

During the whole month of Ramadan, Muslims do not eat or drink during the hours of daylight. This means they must get up before dawn, while it is still dark to have their meal called sahoor. From the moment of the breaking of dawn, Muslims can have neither food nor drink until sunset. Once the sun has set, they can break the fast, which is called iftar.

We Muslims often break our fast by eating a few dates. It is the way of Allah's Messenger (ﷺ).

It is during the month of Ramadan that Allah's Messenger (ﷺ) began to receive the words of the Glorious Qur'an. The Noble Qur'an is Allah's most precious gift to man. The month of Ramadan and fasting during it is the anniversary of the Glorious Qur'an. It is, therefore, the time of thanksgiving. It is the time to thank Allah for all His gifts. It is the time to remember that man should rely on Allah for everything. Fasting teaches self-discipline. It makes us aware of Allah.

Islam teaches us that there is no god but Allah. A Muslim must live a life that is pleasing to Allah. That means putting Allah's Commands before his own desires. When a Muslim fasts, he obeys the Command of Allah and puts Allah's Command before his wants and needs.

Fasting is a shield against evil. It builds up the strength to resist evil that comes in the way of a Muslim. This helps him to say 'no' to the temptations in his everyday life.

Every night, when the fast is broken, the meal is like a celebration. Muslims thank Allah for giving them the power to keep the fast that day. There are people among the Muslims who are not expected to fast. Travellers and those who are sick do not have to fast. They should make up for the missed number of days when they are able to do so.

You will learn about fasting in detail later on, Inshaa Allah.

Exercises

Exercise 1

Answer the following questions.

1. How long is the time of fasting?

   _____

2. In which month did the Prophet () start receiving the words of the Qur'an?

   _____

3. What anniversary does the month of Ramadan mark?

   _____

Exercise 2

Fill in the blanks.

1. Ramadan is the time of _____.

2. Fasting teaches us _____.

3. When a Muslim fasts, he puts Allah's Commands before his

   _____ and _____.

8
Chapter

Hajj is the pilgrimage to the House of Allah – the Ka'bah – in Makkah. It is the fifth pillar of Islam. Hajj requires pilgrims to perform certain acts. These acts are the acts of hajj.

Hajj is compulsory for every adult, sane Muslim, male or female, once in his or her lifetime, provided:

1. He has enough money for the journey,
2. He is in good health,
3. The journey to Makkah is safe and does not involve any danger.

Children may go for hajj with their parents, but it is compulsory for them to perform hajj again when they become adults and are able to do so.

The acts of hajj are as follows:

1. Ihram: the formal intention of performing hajj. A man puts on two pieces of unsewn white cloth and does not cover his head, among other things. A woman should cover everything except for the face and hands.

2. Talbiyah (declaring of one's arrival for hajj).

3. Tawaf – going around the Ka'bah – seven times on arrival at Makkah.

4. Sa'ee – walking seven times back and forth between the two hillocks of Safa and Marwah.

5. Spending the night of 8th Dhul-Hijjah at Mina.

6. Staying in Arafah on the 9th Dhul-Hijjah.

7. Spending the night of 9th Dhul-Hijjah at Muzdalifah.

8. Stoning the Jamratul Aqaba in Mina on the 10th of Dhul-Hijjah.

9. Sacrificing an animal in Mina (depending on the type of hajj one is performing).

10. Shaving the head or having a haircut.

11. Tawaf al–Ifadah: going round the Ka'bah seven times, and performing Sa'ee between Safa and

Marwah, according to the type of hajj one is performing. You will learn about the types of hajj in detail later on, inshaa Allah.

12. Stoning the pillars in Mina, on the 11th, 12th and 13th Dhul-Hijjah. Stoning these pillars on the 13th Dhul-Hijjah is optional.

13. The Farewell Tawaf.

Allah's Messenger (ﷺ) said, 'He who makes a pilgrimage to the House – avoiding indecent and immoral behaviour – will return as pure from sins as the day he was born.' (Al-Bukharee)

He also said that a pilgrimage that is mabroor is better than this world and all it contains. There is no reward for such a pilgrimage but Paradise. (Al-Bukharee)

Mabroor means one that is done with the intention of seeking Allah's pleasure only and done in accordance with the Prophet's Sunnah.

Although visiting the Prophet's Mosque in Madinah is not an act of hajj, it is recommended to do so.

Exercises

Exercise 1

Answer the following questions.

1. What is the reward for a pilgrimage that is mabroor?

   _____

2. What are the three conditions needed for hajj?

   _____

   _____

3. What is the meaning of ihram?

   _____

   _____

Exercise 2

Fill in the blanks.

1. Hajj is the pilgrimage to the _____ in Makkah.

2. Hajj is the _____ pillar of Islam.

3. Tawaf is to go around the Ka'bah _____ times.

Exercises

Exercise 3

Are these statements true or false?

1. If someone is not in good health, he still has to perform hajj.

    _____

2. Women must cover the face while in a state of ihram. _____

3. Shaving the head is an act of hajj. _____

9

Chapter

Allah is the Creator. When you look at the sky, the sun and the moon and the stars, whom do you think of? When you see the flowers, the trees, birds and animals, whom do you think of? Who made the whole world?

Allah made the sun, the moon and the sky, and Allah made the first man. He called him Adam. Man is different from animals and plants in many ways. Animals and plants cannot think the way man thinks. They cannot talk, but Adam could do these things. The Qu'ran mentions Adam about twenty five times in different surahs.

The man Allah made had a body and a soul. Each of the people of the world has a body and a soul.

Allah created Adam from clay and breathed life into him. When our Lord said to the angels, 'I am putting a khaleefah on the earth,' the angels said, 'Why put on it one who will cause corruption and shed blood on it, while we glorify you with praise?' Allah said, 'I know what you do not know.'

Allah then taught Adam the names of all things. Then he asked the angels, 'Tell me the names of these if you are truthful?' They said, 'Glory be to You! We have no knowledge except what You have taught us. You are the All-knowing, the All-wise.'

Allah said, 'Adam, tell them their names.' And Adam told them their names. Allah then commanded the angels to prostrate to Adam. They prostrated but Iblees who was of the jinn did not prostrate. He refused, was arrogant and was one of the disbelievers.

Adam first lived in the Garden of Paradise with his wife Hawwa.

The Garden was very beautiful. Allah allowed Adam and his wife Hawwa to eat freely whatever and whenever they wished. But He forbade them to approach a particular tree in the Garden. He told them to keep away from this tree and warned them not to eat of it, or they would become wrongdoers.

But shaytan made them slip up by whispering evil thoughts into their hearts. He lied to them by telling them that if they ate of that tree, it would make them like angels, and they would live forever.

At last Adam and Hawwa forgot Allah's warning. They ate of the tree. As soon they tasted it, they felt ashamed and knew that they had done something wrong.

They were sorry for disobeying Allah. They prayed to Allah to forgive them, and He forgave them. But Allah commanded them to go to earth to live there for some time. He also promised that they and their children would be allowed to return to Paradise if they obeyed Allah.

Allah also made Adam a Prophet. He was the first Prophet. He worshipped Allah alone. He taught his children and grandchildren how to worship and obey Allah. He also taught his children and grandchildren how to be thankful to Allah.

Adam and Hawwa had many children and grandchildren. After the death of Adam (عَلَيْهِ السَّلَام), Allah chose other Prophets from among the children of Prophet Adam (عَلَيْهِ السَّلَام).

Exercises

Exercise 1

Circle the correct word.

1. Allah created Adam from (fire – clay).

2. (Angels – Iblees] did not bow to Adam (عَلَيْهِ السَّلاَم).

3. Allah (forgave – did not forgive) Adam and Hawwa.

4. Adam was the (last – first) prophet.

5. As soon as Adam and Hawwa ate of the tree, they (felt ashamed – became angels).

6. Iblees was (an angel – one of the jinn).

Exercise 2

Answer these questions.

1. How are plants and animals different from man?

   _____

   _____

2. Why did Allah create Adam?

   _____

   _____

3. Who made Adam (عَلَيْهِ السَّلاَم) disobey Allah?

   _____

10

Chapter

Khadijah ( ) was the daughter of Khuwaylid ibn (son of) Asad. She belonged to the Quraysh tribe.

Khadijah ( ) was the first wife of the Prophet ( ). The Prophet ( ) loved her very much. The wives of the Prophet are called 'Mothers of the Believers', and Khadijah was the first 'mother of the believers'.

The Prophet's marriage to Khadijah ( ) took place about fifteen years before the beginning of the revelation. He was then twenty-five and she was forty-years old. She was a rich widow and ran a large trade of her own. It was Khadijah who offered herself in marriage to the Prophet ( ) when she asked him to do business for her and found out about his good qualities. She remained deeply devoted to him and gave him moral support throughout her life.

Khadijah ( ) had great wealth, a large house in Makkah and a number of maids. She was polite, affectionate and of noble character.

The Prophet (ﷺ) once mentioned that the best of the women of her time was Maryam the mother of the Prophet Isa (عليه السلام), and the best of the women of her time was Khadijah (ﷺ). (Al-Bukhaaree)

She was indeed a very worthy companion of the Last Prophet (ﷺ). He never thought of marrying another woman as long as she lived.

The marriage proved to be one of love and happiness. All the Prophet's sons and daughters, with the exception of Ibraaheem who died as a little boy, were the fruit of this marriage. Khadijah bore the Prophet (ﷺ) two sons: al-Qaasim and Abdullah who both died at a very early age.

She also bore him four daughters. They were:
1. Fatimah,   2. Ruqayyah,
3. Umm Kulthum, and 4. Zaynab.

Khadijah (ﷺ) was the first woman to accept Islam.

Exercises

Exercise 1

Match the following.

A

1. Khadijah (رضي الله عنها) married the Prophet ﷺ
2. She was the daughter
3. Muhammad (ﷺ) married her
4. Khadijah was a
5. The Prophet (ﷺ) used to

B

A at the age of 25.
B trade for Khadijah (رضي الله عنها).
C at the age of 40.
D of Khadijah.
E rich woman.
F of Khuwaylid.

Exercise 2

Are these statements true or false?

1. Khadijah was the second woman to accept Islam. _____

2. She bore the Prophet (ﷺ) two sons. _____

3. She was a poor woman. _____

Exercises

Exercise 3

Answer these questions.

1. Who was the Prophet's first wife?

    _____

    _____

2. What were the Prophet's daughters' names?

    _____

    _____

3. Write a few lines on the character of Khadijah (ﷺ).

    _____

    _____

    _____

    _____

11

Chapter

A long time ago, in Babylon in Iraq, there lived a man called Azar. He was very popular. He was a seller of idols. He made idols with his own hands. He bowed down before these idols. He worshipped them.

Azar had a son called Ibraaheem. He was born in Babylon. He was very intelligent. Ibraaheem (عَلَيْهِ السَّلاَم) saw the people bowing down before idols. He was amazed. He knew idols were made of stone. They could not speak. They could not hear. They could not eat. He knew they could not help nor harm anybody. He saw flies sit on them. The idols could not send the flies away. Ibraaheem (عَلَيْهِ السَّلاَم) saw mice eat from the food which lay before the idols. The idols could not stop the mice from eating this food.

Ibraaheem (عليه السلام) wondered, 'Why do people worship idols? Why do people ask idols for help?'

Ibraaheem (عليه السلام) would ask his father, 'Why do you worship idols? Why do you bow down before them? The idols cannot speak. They cannot hear. They cannot help anyone. They cannot eat nor drink. Why do you then put food and drink before them?'

Azar would become angry. He did not know what to say. He did not have any answers to these questions.

Ibraaheem (عليه السلام) gave the same advice to his people. They did not have any answers to his questions either. One day Ibraaheem (عليه السلام) went to the temple where idols were kept. He asked the idols, 'There is food and drink lying before you. Why don't you eat? Why don't you drink? Why are you all so silent? Why don't you speak?' The idols were silent. They were made of stones. Stones of course, do not speak.

Ibraaheem (عليه السلام) became angry. He grabbed an axe. He began to hit the idols with the axe. He smashed them all except the big one. Instead, he hung the axe around its neck.

When the people came to worship and bow down before their idols, they were dumbfounded and very angry. They could not believe what they saw.

'Who has done this to our gods?' they cried.

They had heard Ibraaheem (عليه السلام) talk about the idols. They brought him to the building and asked him, 'Are you the one who has done this to our gods?'

Ibraaheem (عليه السلام) pointed to the largest unbroken idol and calmly said, 'But this, their chief has done it. Ask him if he is able to speak.'

The people knew the idols were made of stones. They knew stones do not hear nor speak. They knew the largest idol was also made of stone. It could not move from its place. How could it break the other idols? The people were confused. They said, 'Ibraaheem, you know that idols cannot speak.' Now was the turn of Ibraaheem (عَلَيْهِ السَّلَام). He asked them, 'How can you worship idols made of stone when they can neither help nor harm you? Why don't you understand?'

The people fell silent. They had no answer. But they met together. Ibraaheem (عَلَيْهِ السَّلَام) had broken the idols. He had insulted their gods. They decided to punish him. They lit a huge fire and threw Ibraaheem (عَلَيْهِ السَّلَام) into it. But Allah saved Ibraaheem (عَلَيْهِ السَّلَام). He commanded the fire, 'Be coolness and safety upon Ibraaheem.' (21:69).' So it was!

The people saw that the fire did not harm Ibraaheem (عَلَيْهِ السَّلَام). They saw that the flames and heat did not harm him at all. He was safe and sound.

Exercises

Exercise 1

Choose from the following words and fill in the blanks.

[seller, burn, Babylon, idols, stones]

1.   Azar lived in _____ in Iraq.

2.   He was a maker and _____ of idols.

3.   The people of Ibraaheem (العليه السلام) worshipped _____.

4.   The people decided to _____ Ibraaheem (العليه السلام) alive.

5.   Idols are made of _____ or wood.

Exercise 2

Answer the following questions.

1.   Why was Azar popular?

_____

2.   Why did Ibraaheem (العليه السلام) not worship the idols?

_____

_____

Exercises

3.   How did the people react when they went to the temple?

_____

_____

Exercise 3

Explain how the fire did not harm Ibraaheem (عليه السلام).

_____

_____

_____

_____

Prophet Ibraaheem (ﷺ) had two sons. Both of them became famous because Allah made them prophets. The first of them was Isma'eel, the sacrificed one. His mother's name was Haajar.

Isma'eel (ﷺ) was the first son born to Prophet Ibraaheem (ﷺ) in answer to his prayers. Ibraaheem (ﷺ) prayed to Allah to give him a righteous child, and Allah gave him the good news of a forbearing boy.

It was Isma'eel (ﷺ) whom Allah asked Ibraaheem (ﷺ) to sacrifice. Ibraaheem and Isma'eel were both put to the test. This happened when Isma'eel (ﷺ) was only thirteen years old. It was also Isma'eel (ﷺ) who went with his parents, Ibraaheem and Haajar, while he was only an infant, to the valley known today as Makkah.

Ibraaheem (ﷺ) left them there with only a small quantity of water and food. He put his trust in Allah to help and protect them. He left them under a tree at the place where Makkah stands today. Haajar sat in its shadow with the child on her lap. Around her there was nothing but sand and rocky slopes. How good the shade of the tree was!

There was a horrible silence all around, without any living thing! No birds, no animals! The night passed, and another day, and another night.

When there was no more water left, the child began to cry. Haajar cried out to the Lord. Frightened by the suffering of her thirsty child, she ran to and fro through the valley, between the two hills of Safa and Marwah to see if she could see anybody.

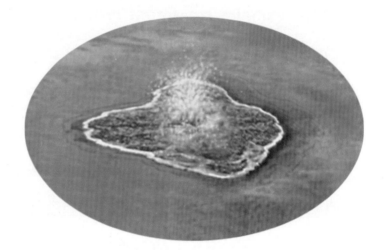

While in this desperate situation, Angel Jibreel (عَلَيْهِ السَّلَام) appeared and hit the earth with his heel. A stream of water gushed forth and began to flow over the sand. Haajar shouted with joy. She pressed the child's face into the cool water so that he might drink. She also drank with him. She heaped a little wall of sand around the spring. It became a well. This blessed well is known as the Well of Zamzam and exists to this day.

When Ibraaheem (عليه السلام) returned to the valley after some time, he found Haajar and Isma'eel alive, as Allah had promised him. Later, Prophet Ibraaheem (عليه السلام) built the Ka'bah with the help of

Isma'eel. When Isma'eel grew up, Ibraaheem (عليه السلام) and Isma'eel (عليه السلام) were both put to another test. When

Isma'eel (عليه السلام) was old enough to work with him, Ibraaheem (عليه السلام) said, 'My son, I saw in a dream that I must sacrifice you; what do you think about this?' Isma'eel (عليه السلام) answered, 'Do as you are ordered, father. Allah willing, you will find me firm.' Then when they had both submitted and Ibraaheem (عليه السلام) had laid Isma'eel (عليه السلام) face down on the ground, Allah called out to him, 'Ibraaheem, you have fulfilled the dream.'

Allah then commanded Ibraaheem to sacrifice a ram in his place.

We are very grateful to both Prophet Ibraaheem (عليه السلام) and Isma'eel (عليه السلام) for their noble example. Muslims all over the world sacrifice animals on the day of Eed al-Adha in memory of Ibraaheem's readiness to sacrifice Isma'eel to Allah to this day, and that will continue till the end of the world.

Exercises

Exercise 1

Match side A to side B

	A		B
1	Ibraaheem had	a	with Zamzam.
2	Allah helped Haajar	b	two sons
3	Ibraaheem left his family	c	Safa and Marwah.
4	Haajar ran between	d	a prophet.
5	Isma'eel was	e	in the care of Allah.
		f	one son.

Exercises

Exercise 2

Describe what Makkah looked like when Ibraaheem (عليه السلام) left his family there.

_____

_____

_____

_____

Exercise 3

Complete the following.

1. Isma'eel's parents were _____ and _____.

2. Ibraaheem (عليه السلام) left his family _____.

3. Isma'eel (عليه السلام) answered, 'Do as you are _____, father'.

4. Isma'eel (عليه السلام) helped Ibraaheem (عليه السلام) _____.

5. Ibraaheem's obedience to sacrifice his son put an end to

_____.

Exercises

Exercise 4

Are these statements true of false?

1. At the time of sacrifice, Isma'eel was ten. _____

2. Muslims sacrifice in memory of Ibraaheem's readiness to sacrifice Isma'eel to Allah. _____

3. Isma'eel refused to obey his father. _____

Chapter 13

Prophet Ibraaheem (عليه السلام) had two sons. The eldest was Isma'eel whose mother was Haajar. Ishaq was his second son born of his other wife Sarah.

The Qur'an tells us in Surat Hud how the good news of the birth of Ishaq was given to Prophet Ibraaheem (عليه السلام).

Allah sent some angels to him to give him the good news of a birth in his family, because Prophet Ibraaheem (عليه السلام) had no children from his wife Sarah, and for this reason she felt sad. Both Ibraaheem (عليه السلام) and his wife Sarah had become old. There was no hope for them to have children. The angels gave the good news of the birth of Ishaq to Sarah and Ibraaheem (عليه السلام). They also gave them the good news of the birth of their grandson Ya'qub in their lives. Both Ishaq and Ya'qub became messengers of Allah of great standing.

These angels came to Prophet Ibraaheem (ﷺ) in human form. He took them as normal guests. He brought a dish of roasted calf and placed it before them. Because they were angels and had no desire of eating and drinking, they did not spread their hands towards it.

Ibraaheem (ﷺ) was a hundred years old when Ishaq was born. But when Isma'eel was born to him he was eighty seven-years old.

Exercises

Exercise 1

Answer the following questions.

1. How did Ibraaheem (عليه السلام) honour his special guests?

_____

_____

2. How old was Ibraaheem (عليه السلام) when Ishaq was born?

_____

Exercise 2

Name the following:

1. Ibraaheem's children   : _____
2. Ibraaheem's guests   : _____
3. Sarah's grandson   : _____
4. Ishaq's parents   : _____

14

Chapter

Water is a great gift from Allah. It is the essence of life. From water Allah made every living creature. Water preserves the body's moisture. Without it, there would be no life on earth.

Water helps in the digestion of food and helps cleanse the body of toxins.

The goodness and purity of water can usually be seen in three ways:

1. From its colour, which should be clear;
2. From its smell, that it should have no smell at all;
3. From its taste, that it should not be completely changed.

The water of Zamzam is without doubt the noblest of all kinds of water. It is the most pleasing to souls. It is the most valued by people.

When a Muslim becomes ritually impure by breaking wind, for example, he cleanses himself with pure water. When he wishes to take a bath, he bathes himself with pure water. When his clothes become unclean, he washes them with pure water. When the floor becomes unclean, he washes it with pure water.

Rainwater, spring water, ice water and river water are different kinds of pure water. Water remains pure as long as its colour, taste or smell does not change.

A Muslim washes himself with pure water. He makes wudhu with pure water. He washes his clothes with pure water.

Exercises

Exercise 1

Answer the following questions.

1.   How would we know if water is pure?

_____

_____

2.   Name the different types of water.

_____

_____

3.   Write down any five uses of pure water.

_____

_____

_____

Exercise 2

Name the following:

1.   The essence of life   : _____

2.   The noblest of all kinds of water : _____

3.   The Giver of water   : _____

Exercises

Exercise 3

Fill in the blanks.

1.   Allah made every living creature from _____.

2.   Water _____ the food and causes it to _____.

3.   Pure water benefits the _____ as well as the _____.

4.   The water of _____ is without doubt the noblest of all kinds of water.

Urine is impure. If urine stains anything, it becomes impure. If your clothes are stained with urine, they are impure. A Muslim cannot offer salah if his clothes are impure. He has to make them pure by washing them.

Stool is also impure. Things stained with stool become impure. Water purifies the clothes and the body.

If a part of your body is stained with urine or stool, it becomes impure. Washing with water the part of the body stained with urine or stool makes it pure.

Remember, cleanliness is a part of faith.

Exercises

Exercise 1

Answer the following questions.

1.   Mention two things that are impure.

_____

_____

2.   What makes impure things pure?

_____

_____

3.   What will you do if a baby wets your clothes?

_____

_____

Exercise 2

Make a chart on cleanliness and put it up in your classroom.

Tahaarah is an Arabic word. It means purity. Tahaarah in Islam means the state of cleanliness which a Muslim needs to be able to perform certain acts of worship. If a person has tahaarah, he becomes clean in his body and clothes. But keep in mind that the main purpose of tahaarah is cleanliness of the heart and mind.

The things which break tahaarah

If you are in a state of tahaarah, your tahaarah will break if any of the following things happen to you. They are called al-hadath al-asghar, or the minor defilement and require wudhu to regain purity.

1. breaking wind
2. passing urine
3. passing stool
4. deep sleep

A Muslim cannot offer salah if he is not in a state of purity – tahaarah. Allah will not accept our salah if we offer it in a state of impurity.

Remember if any of the things mentioned above (al-hadath al-asghar) happens to anyone of us, we are not allowed to perform salah. We must regain the proper state of tahaarah. The tahaarah may be regained by making wudhu, tayammum or ghusl (a complete bath).

You will learn about these in detail later on, inshaa Allah.

Exercises

Exercise 1

1. List some of the things that break tahaarah.

   _____

   _____

2. Explain the meaning of tahaarah.

   _____

   _____

Exercise 2

Fill in the blanks.

1. Tahaarah is the cleanliness of _____ and _____.

2. Tahaarah may be regained by making _____ ,
   _____ or _____.

3. A Muslim cannot offer his _____ if he is not pure.

If you relieve yourself or break wind, you become ritually impure.

If you relieve yourself, you should clean yourself well and then make wudhu before offering salah.

If you break wind, just make wudhu before you offer salah.

It is necessary to perform wudhu before offering salah. After making wudhu, a Muslim may offer his salah. Allah's Messenger (ﷺ) said, 'Allah does not accept the salah of any one of you who does not make wudhu after he becomes ritually impure.'

(Al-Bukhaaree and Muslim)

Exercise

Answer the following questions.

1. When should a Muslim perform wudhu?

   _____

   _____

2. When does a Muslim become ritually impure?

   _____

   _____

3. Whose prayer does Allah not accept?

   _____

   _____

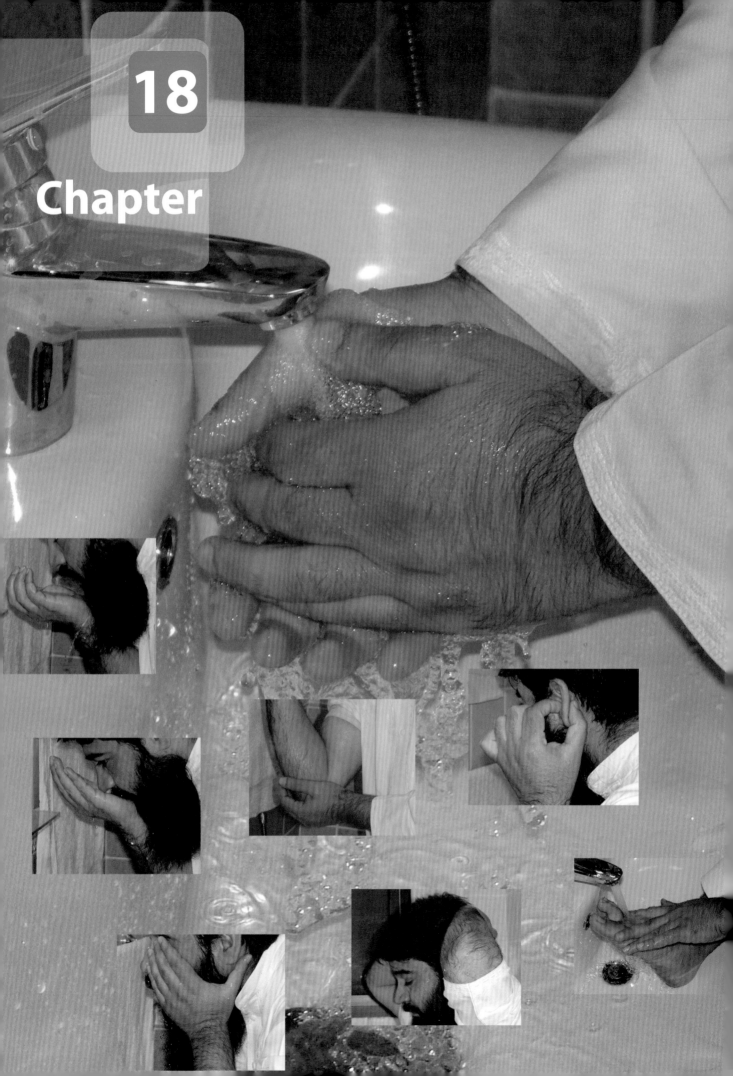

Niyyah in Wudhu

In Islam, any good action, which is done without the correct intention will not be accepted by Allah. It is therefore very important that whatever we do, we should do it to please Allah. All our acts of worship should be done for Allah alone and according to the teachings of the Prophet (ﷺ).

The Prophet Muhammad (ﷺ) said that a person's prayer (salah) is not accepted without wudhu. So, before praying a Muslim must purify himself. A Muslim should also make sure that his clothes and the place where he wants to pray is clean.

Wudhu should be performed with pure water.

The way to perform wudhu:

1. Make the intention of purifying yourself for worship.
2. Start in the name of Allah by saying: بِسْمِ الله
   Bismillaah (In the name of Allah).
3. Wash the right hand and the left hand three times. You should wash up to the wrists and between the fingers.
4. Rinse the mouth three times.

5. Sniff water into the nose and give it a gentle blow, three times.

6. Wash the face three times, from the hairline to the chin and from ear to ear.

7. Wash the right forearm up to the elbow including the hand three times. Then wash the left forearm up to the elbow including the hand three times.

8. Wet your hands and wipe the head once from the hairline to the neck and back again to the front.

9. Wipe the inside and outside parts of the ears, once.

10. Wash the feet starting with the right foot. Do this three times. Remember to rub between the toes and wash the heels and the ankles.

11. Now recite ash-Shahadah.

أَشْهَدُ أَنْ لَا إِلهَ إِلَّا اللهُ وَحْدَهُ لَا شَرِيكَ لَهُ وَأَ شْهَدُ أَنَّ مُحَمَّداً عَبْدُهُ وَرَسُولُه

ash-hadu allaa ilaaha illallaahu wahdahu laa shareeka lahu wa ash-hadu anna muhammadan 'abduhu warasooluh.

I bear witness that there is no god worthy of worship except Allah, alone without any partners, and I bear witness that Muhammad is His servant and Messenger.

Exercise

Read the following passage carefully and then answer the question that follows.

Aminah decided to get ready for prayer. She was in a hurry and had to get back to her homework. She started to do her wudhu without mentioning the name of Allah. She carried on with it but when she washed her forearms, the water did not touch her elbows. She finished and hurriedly put on her scarf and began her salah.

What mistakes did Aminah make in her wudhu?

_____

_____

_____

_____

19

Chapter

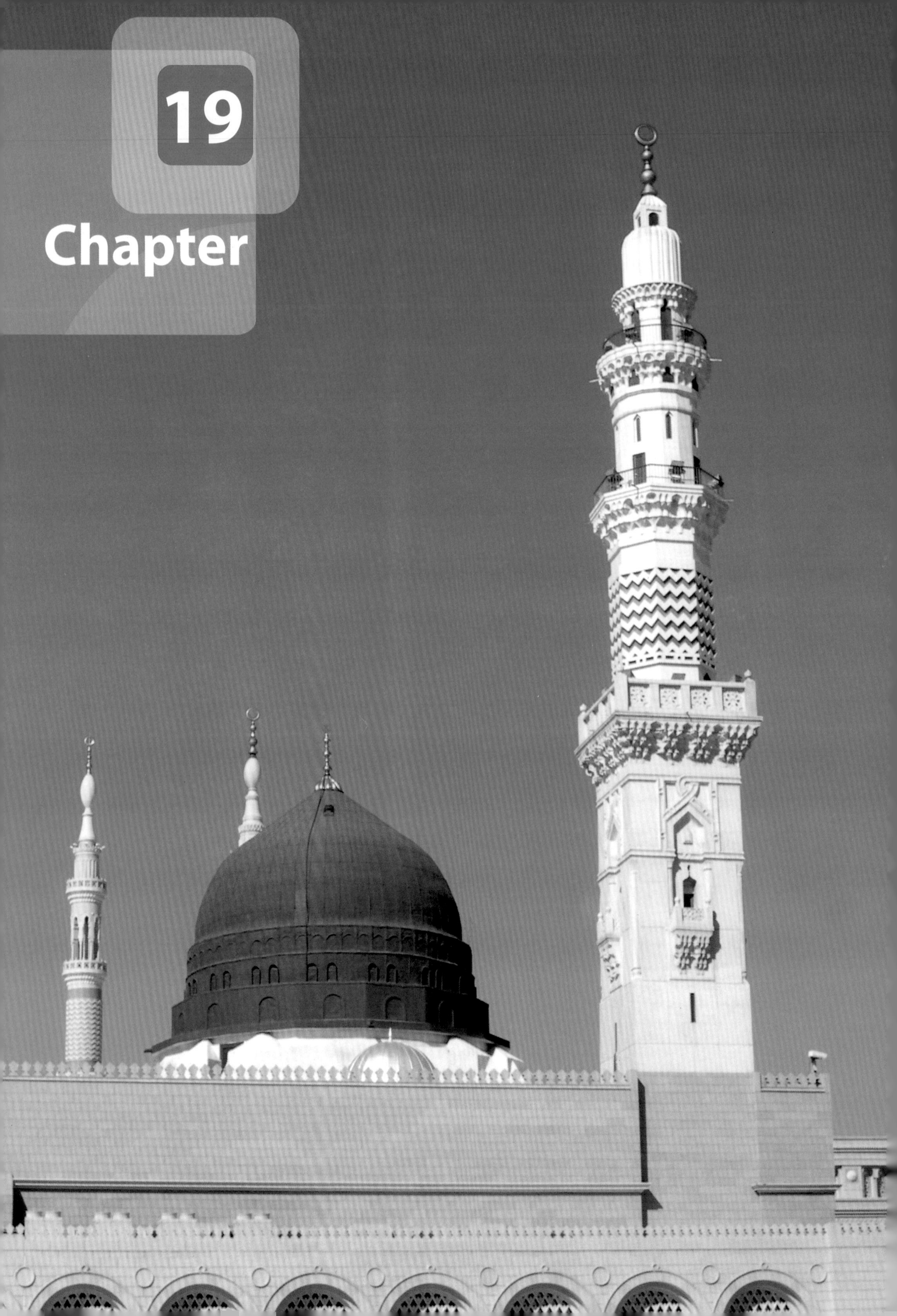

Supporter of the poor

Allah's Messenger (ﷺ) had become very popular in the whole of Arabia. Everyone respected and honoured him; his wisdom, honesty and trustworthiness were the talk of the country. He had no enemy throughout Arabia. He was a trader by profession. He spent his life in ease after his marriage with Khadijah (رضي الله عنها).

Once famine broke out, and there was a serious shortage of food in the country. Abu Talib had a big family to support. He was the head of the clan of Banu Hashim. He passed his days in want and poverty.

Having seen his bad condition, the Prophet (ﷺ) went to his uncle Al-Abbas ibn Abdul-Muttalib and told him about the famine and the difficulties that Abu Talib was facing. He further said that it would be better if they each took one of Abu Talib's sons under their care. Al-Abbas agreed and both of them went to Abu Talib and expressed their desire. Abu Talib happily agreed. So the Prophet (ﷺ) took Ali and Al-Abbas took Ja'far.

This happened in the same year the Ka'bah was rebuilt.

Exercises

Exercise 1

Give reasons.

1. Everyone respected the Prophet (ﷺ).

    _____

    _____

2. The Prophet (ﷺ) went to speak to Al-Abbas.

    _____

    _____

3. The Prophet (ﷺ) started taking care of Ali.

    _____

    _____

Exercise 2

Are these statements true or false?

1. Abu Talib and Al-Abbas were brothers. _____

2. Al-Abbas took care of Ali. _____

3. The Prophet (ﷺ) supported the poor. _____

Chapter 20

Khadijah (﵂) had a nephew. His name was Hakeem ibn Haram. Hakeem had bought a slave and offered him to Khadijah (﵂) and she offered him to the Prophet (ﷺ). It was this slave who was known as Zayd ibn Harithah.

Before Islam, Zayd was taken during a raid and sold as a slave. When Zayd's father, Harithah, and his uncle Ka'b came to know that Zayd was living with the Prophet (ﷺ) in Makkah as his slave, both of them came to Makkah and requested the Prophet (ﷺ) to set Zayd free. The Prophet (ﷺ) accepted their request at once. He said that Zayd was free to go with them if he so desired.

Zayd was then called, and the Prophet (ﷺ) asked him, 'Do you know these two men?' Zayd replied, 'Yes! They are my father and uncle.' He then said, 'They have come to take you back with them. I give you permission to go with them.'

Zayd replied, 'I do not want to go with them.' Zayd's father scolded him and said, 'Do you prefer slavery to freedom?' Zayd replied, 'I have seen in Muhammad (ﷺ) such wonderful things that I can prefer no one in the entire world to him.'

Having heard Zayd's reply, the Prophet (ﷺ) got up, took Zayd with him and, entering the Ka'bah, said in a loud voice, 'O people! Be witness to it that today I set Zayd free and take him as my son.' This delighted both the father and uncle of Zayd and they went away, leaving their son in the company of the Prophet (ﷺ).

From that day on, the boy came to be called Zayd ibn Muhammad instead of Zayd ibn Harithah until Allah's Command came to the contrary. So he returned to the name Zayd ibn Harithah. But he still enjoyed the love, affection and the great company of the Prophet (ﷺ).

Exercise

Answer these questions.

1. What was Zayd's father's name?

    _____

2. Did Zayd (رضي الله عنه) want to go back with his father? Why?

    _____

    _____

3. Was Harithah happy that his son stayed with the Prophet
    (ﷺ)? Why?

    _____

    _____

When Allah's Messenger (ﷺ) was 32 or 33 years of age, he started enjoying solitude. He felt a unique joy in this solitude. He naturally disliked idol worship. He never ate food offered to idols.

During this time, Allah's Messenger (ﷺ) would think deeply about Allah's powers and would glorify and praise Him. The more he was drawing near the age of forty, the more he loved solitude. He would often go to the Cave of Hira, taking with him food and water to pray to Allah in perfect peace and privacy. He would return when he run short of supplies.

The Cave of Hira is in Mount An-Noor (Mount of Light), which is two miles away from Makkah towards the north on the way to Mina. The cave is four yards long and about three quarters of a yard wide. During those days he had true dreams.

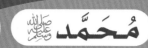

Exercise 1

Fill in the blanks.

1. The Prophet (ﷺ) felt a _____ joy in this solitude.

2. During this time, he would think deeply about Allah's _____ and would _____ and _____ Him.

3. During those days, the Prophet (ﷺ) had true _____ .

Exercise 2

Answer these questions.

1. Was the Prophet (ﷺ) happy that his people worshipped idols?

    _____

2. What would he do in the Cave of Hira?

    _____

    _____

22
Chapter

Allah's Messenger (ﷺ) loved going into retreat. He was happy when he could be on his own. He used to walk away from Makkah until he was well out of sight of the houses. He usually went to the Cave of Hira. He would remain there for several days and nights in a row. He would take with him enough food and drink to last for that time. He would worship and pray in the manner of Prophet Ibraaheem (ﷺ). He followed the pure human need to turn to Allah.

The Prophet (ﷺ) would be alone in the cave most of the time. Khadijah's servants would provide him with food and drink and other basic needs. She herself would visit him from time to time and would sometimes bring along his little daughters. His male children had all died when they were very young. The favourite time of the Prophet's staying in the Cave of Hira was the month of Ramadan. He would spend the whole month there in worship.

Allah's Messenger (ﷺ) was once alone in the Cave of Hira. He was forty years old. It was the month of Ramadan in the year 610 C.E.

Suddenly, Angel Jibreel (عليه السلام) appeared to him and said, 'Read!'

'I cannot read,' he answered.

Later, describing what had happened, he said, 'He seized me and squeezed me as hard as I could bear and then let go of me and said, "Read!"

I said, "I cannot read."

Then he squeezed me as hard as I could bear a second time and let go of me. Again he said, "Read!" Then he squeezed me a third time and let go of me and said,

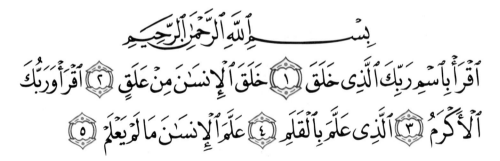

'read in the name of your Lord Who created. He created man from a blood clot. Read, and your Lord is the Most Generous, Who has taught by the pen; He has taught man that which he knew not.'" (96: 1-5)

This was the first day of his Prophethood, and these were the first verses of the Qur'an to be sent to the Messenger of Allah (ﷺ).

Having said this, the angel disappeared. Frightened, Allah's Messenger (ﷺ) went back home. He went to his wife Khadijah (﵂) and said, 'Wrap me up!' Khadijah wrapped him up in a blanket. When he regained peace of mind after a short while, he told Khadijah (﵂) about what had happened to him and said, 'I fear for my life.'

Exercises

Exercise 1

Fill in the blanks.

1. Allah's Messenger (ﷺ) loved going into _____ .

2. He usually went to the Cave of _____ .

3. Later on, Khadijah (ﷺ) _____ him up in a blanket and he told her what had _____ to him.

Exercise 2

Answer these questions.

1. What was the name of the angel who came to Prophet Muhammad (ﷺ)?

    _____

2. What is the name of the cave he used to go to?

    _____

3. Why would he go to this cave?

    _____

23
Chapter

Naturally, Allah's Messenger (ﷺ) was frightened by the experience. He did not know what was happening. He had never heard of anything like this taking place.

Khadijah (﵂) was an intelligent noble lady. She had heard of Prophethood. She had heard about the Prophets and angels. She used to visit her cousin, Waraqah ibn Nawfal. Waraqah was a learned man who had read many books.

Khadijah (﵂) knew the character of Allah's Messenger (ﷺ). She was his wife and was close to his thoughts. She was very well aware of his noble qualities. She felt that Allah's Messenger (ﷺ) had been given Allah's support. She said to the Prophet (ﷺ) with confidence, 'Allah will never disgrace you. You keep good relations with your relatives; you support the weak; you help the poor and the needy; you entertain guests, and you endure hardships in the path of truthfulness.'

Khadijah (رضي الله عنها) then decided to consult her cousin, the learned Waraqah ibn Nawfal. She took the Prophet (ﷺ) to see him. When Waraqah heard what the Prophet (ﷺ) had seen, he said, 'By the One in whose Hand my soul is, you are the Prophet of this nation. That was the same angel who was sent to Musa. I wish I could live up to the time when your people will drive you out.'

Allah's Messenger (عليه السلام) was surprised at what Waraqah had said. He was astonished about the Quraysh driving him out of Makkah, because he knew his own position among them. They all called him the Truthful and the Trustworthy.

He asked, 'Will the people drive me out?'

'Yes,' Waraqah answered, 'No man has ever brought anything like what you have brought without his people rejecting him and fighting him. I'm already old now. If I'm alive on that day, I will give you support.'

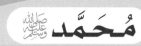
Afterwards, the Prophet (ﷺ) kept visiting the Cave of Hira. But no revelation came to him for some time. One day, while he was walking, he heard a voice from the sky. He looked up and saw the same angel who had visited him in the Cave of Hira. This time he was sitting on a chair between the earth and the sky. He got frightened and hurried back home. He asked his wife Khadijah (ﷺ) to cover him. Then Allah revealed the following verses:

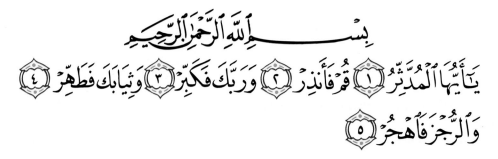

O you covered in garments, arise and warn; and glorify your Lord; and purify your clothing, and keep away from the idols." (74:1-5)

From then on, the revelation kept coming after short intervals. One day, Angel Jibreel (ﷺ), the Trustworthy Spirit, took the Prophet (ﷺ) to the foot of a hill and performed wudhu before him. The Prophet (ﷺ) did the same. Afterwards, Jibreel (ﷺ) led the Prophet (ﷺ) in prayer.

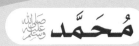

Exercises

Exercise 1

Fill in the blanks.

1. The Prophet's experience in the cave made him _____ .

2. Khadijah (ﷺ) was an _____ lady.

3. She was aware of his _____ qualities.

4. The Trustworthy _____ is Angel Jibreel (عليه السلام).

Exercise 2

Are these statements true or false?

1. Khadijah (ﷺ) gave the Prophet (ﷺ) a lot of support. _____

2. Waraqah ibn Nawfal was Khadijah's uncle. _____

3. Jibreel (عليه السلام) never came back again to the Prophet (ﷺ) after revelation stopped for some time. _____

Activity

In which surah can you find the verses mentioned in this lesson?

24

Chapter

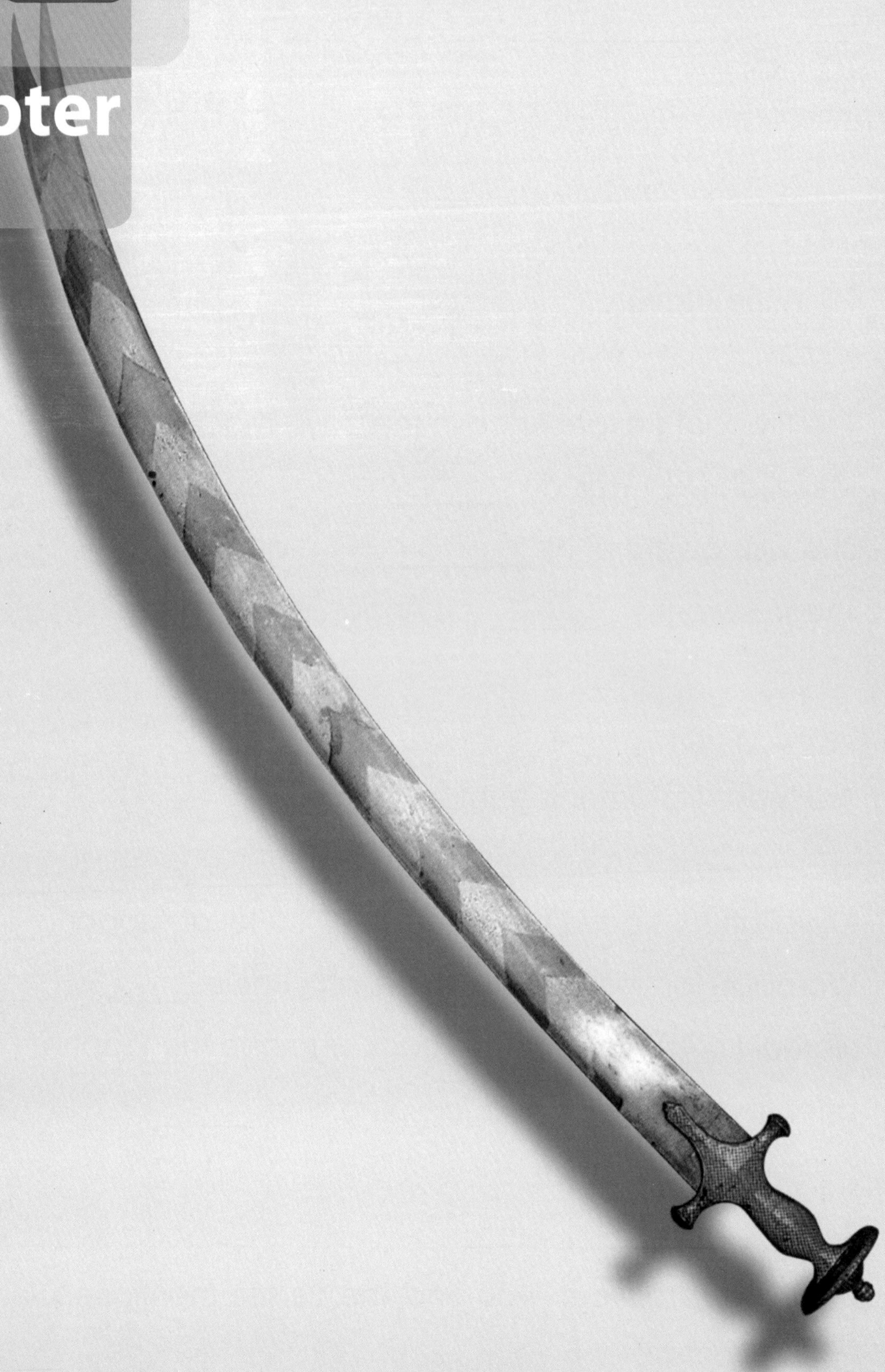

Ali (ﷺ) was the son of Abu Talib. Abu Talib was the Prophet's uncle.

Abu Talib looked after the Prophet (ﷺ) when he was young. Once famine broke out in Arabia. There was a serious shortage of food in the country. Abu Talib had a big family to support. He was the head of the clan of Banu Hashim. He passed his days in want and poverty. The Prophet (ﷺ) took Ali, one of the sons of Abu Talib, under his care. He wanted to help Abu Talib when he ran into difficulty.

Ali (ﷺ) was only ten years old when he accepted Islam, and it was about this time that the Prophet (ﷺ) received the revelation. The Prophet (ﷺ) invited him to accept Islam, and Ali (ﷺ) became a Muslim. Ali (ﷺ) lived with the Prophet (ﷺ). He liked the Prophet (ﷺ) very much.

The Prophet (ﷺ) married his daughter Fatimah to Ali (ﷺ), and they became the parents of Al-Hasan and Al-Husayn, the grandsons of the Prophet (ﷺ).

Exercises

Exercise 1

Name the following:

1. Ali's father _____.

2. The grandsons of the Prophet (ﷺ) from his daughter Fatimah (ﷺ): _____and _____.

Exercise 2

Answer these questions.

1. How old was Ali (ﷺ) when he accepted Islam?

    _____

2. Why did the Prophet (ﷺ) take Ali (ﷺ) under his care?

    _____

    _____

3. Who were the parents of Al-Hasan and Al-Husayn?

    _____

25

Chapter

Ja'far ibn Abee Talib (رضي الله عنه) was the son of Abu Talib. He was a brother of Ali (رضي الله عنه). He was ten years older than Ali. He was one of the earliest Muslims. He was a very brave fighter. He lost both his arms in one battle. The Prophet (ﷺ) called him At-Tayyaar (The Flyer). The Prophet's Companions called him Dhul-Janaahayn (the two-winged one).

The Prophet (ﷺ) once said that he would be given two wings in Paradise.

May Allah be pleased with him.

Exercises

Exercise 1

Answer these questions.

1. Was Ja'far (رضي الله عنه) the cousin of Ali (رضي الله عنه)?

   _____

2. What happened to Ja'far (رضي الله عنه) in one battle?

   _____

   _____

3. Who called him At-Tayyaar?

   _____

4. What does At-Tayyaar mean?

   _____

Exercise 2

Are these statements true or false?

1. Ali (رضي الله عنه) was ten years younger than Ja'far (رضي الله عنه). _____

2. The Prophet (ﷺ) called Ja'far (رضي الله عنه) Dhul-Janaahayn. _____

3. The Prophet (ﷺ) said that Ja'far (رضي الله عنه) would be given two thrones in Paradise. _____